PHANTOM OF THE OPERA
MEDLEY FOR VIOLIN AND PIANO

ARRANGED BY

Lindsey Stirling

The musical works contained in this edition may not be publicly performed
in a dramatic form or context except under license from
The Really Useful Group Limited, 22 Tower Street, London WC2H9TW

ISBN 978-1-4764-7126-4

HAL•LEONARD®
CORPORATION
7777 W. BLUEMOUND RD. P.O. BOX 13819 MILWAUKEE, WI 53213

Visit Hal Leonard Online at
www.halleonard.com

PHANTOM OF THE OPERA MEDLEY

Violin

Music by ANDREW LLOYD WEBBER
Lyrics by CHARLES HART
Additional Lyrics by RICHARD STILGOE and MIKE BATT
Violin arranged by Lindsey Stirling

THINK OF ME
Music by ANDREW LLOYD WEBBER
Lyrics by CHARLES HART
Additional Lyrics by RICHARD STILGOE

THE MUSIC OF THE NIGHT
Music by ANDREW LLOYD WEBBER
Lyrics by CHARLES HART
Additional Lyrics by RICHARD STILGOE

THE PHANTOM OF THE OPERA

Quicker, with intensity (♩ = 158)

ANGEL OF MUSIC
Music by ANDREW LLOYD WEBBER
Lyrics by CHARLES HART
Additional Lyrics by RICHARD STILGOE

PHANTOM OF THE OPERA
MEDLEY FOR VIOLIN AND PIANO

ARRANGED BY

Lindsey Stirling

Cover photo by Devin Graham

ISBN 978-1-4764-7126-4

HAL•LEONARD®
CORPORATION
7777 W. BLUEMOUND RD. P.O. BOX 13819 MILWAUKEE, WI 53213

Visit Hal Leonard Online at
www.halleonard.com

PHANTOM OF THE OPERA MEDLEY

Music by ANDREW LLOYD WEBBER
Lyrics by CHARLES HART
Additional Lyrics by RICHARD STILGOE and MIKE BATT
Violin arranged by Lindsey Stirling
Piano arranged by David Russell

THE PHANTOM OF THE OPERA

Somberly (♩ = 90)

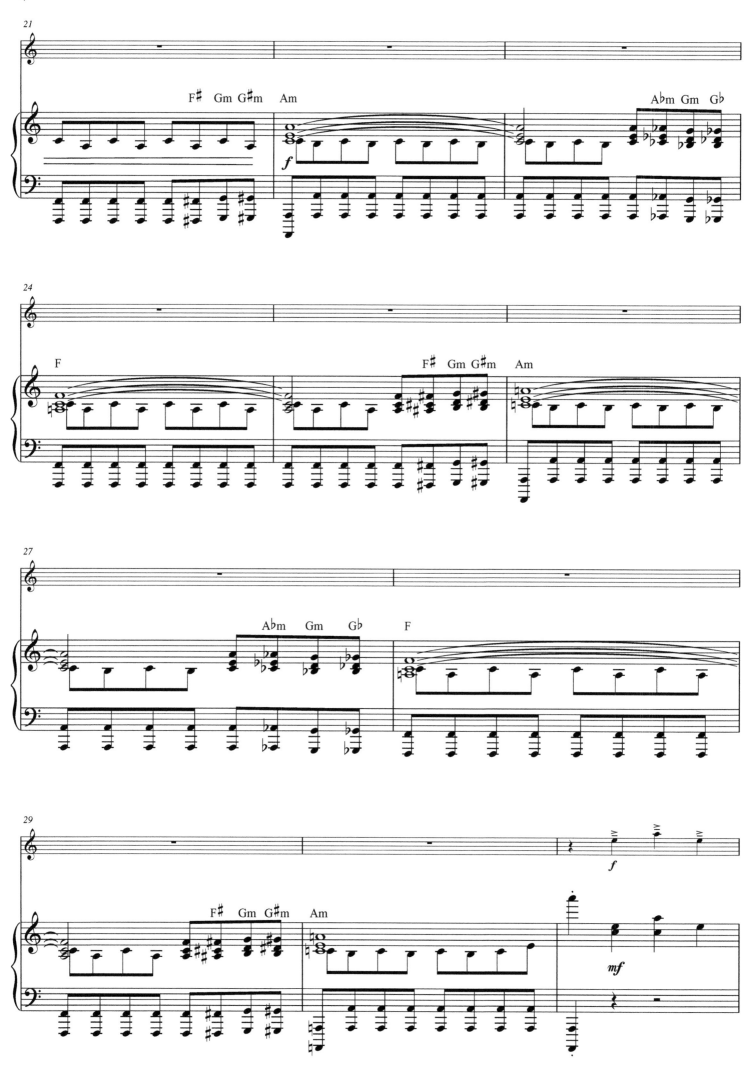

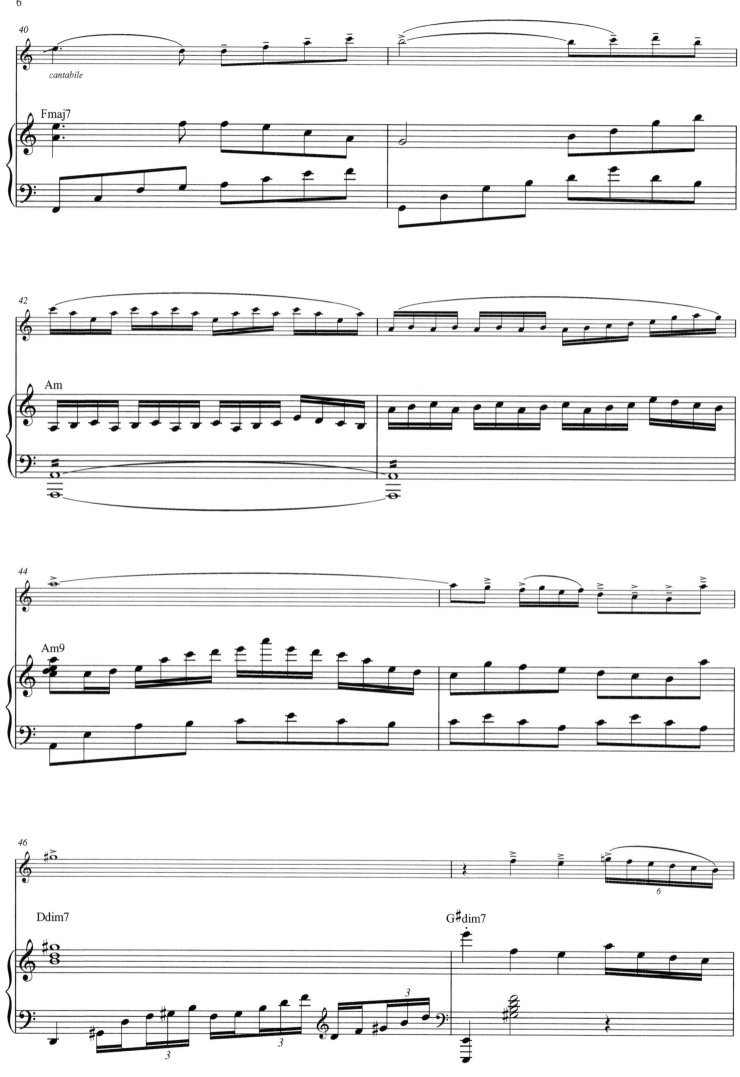

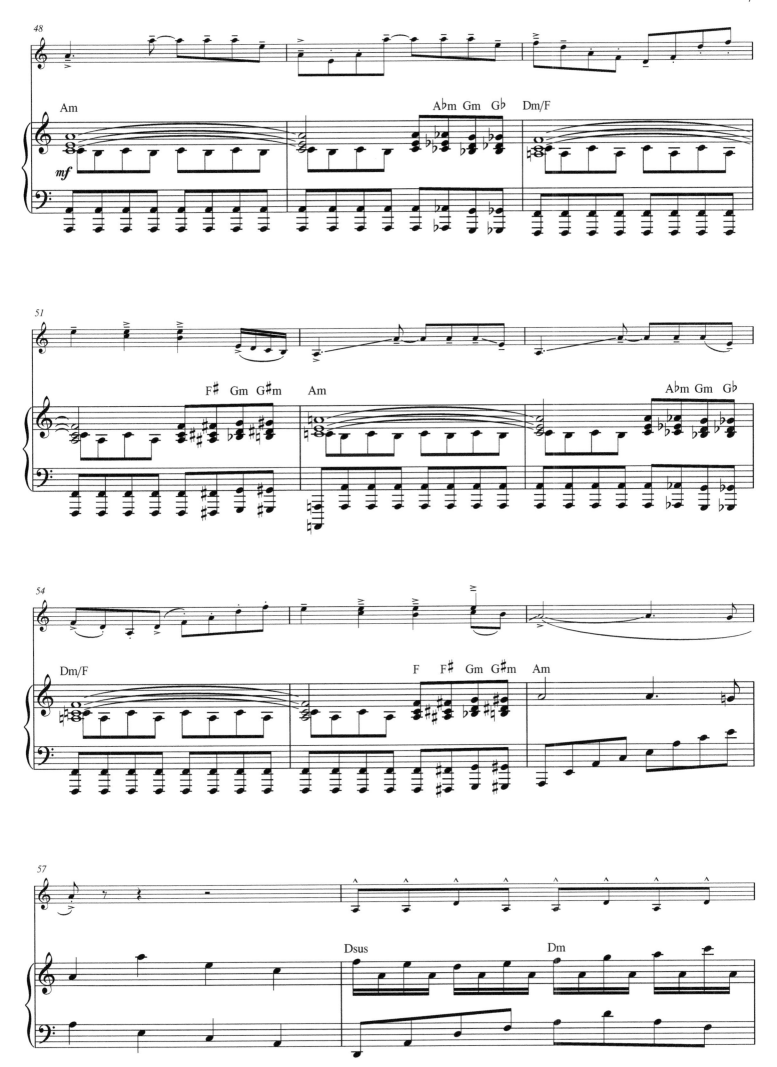

ANGEL OF MUSIC
Music by ANDREW LLOYD WEBBER
Lyrics by CHARLES HART
Additional Lyrics by RICHARD STILGOE

THINK OF ME
Music by ANDREW LLOYD WEBBER
Lyrics by CHARLES HART
Additional Lyrics by RICHARD STILGOE

THE MUSIC OF THE NIGHT
Music by ANDREW LLOYD WEBBER
Lyrics by CHARLES HART
Additional Lyrics by RICHARD STILGOE

Driving forward, with intensity (♩ = 133)

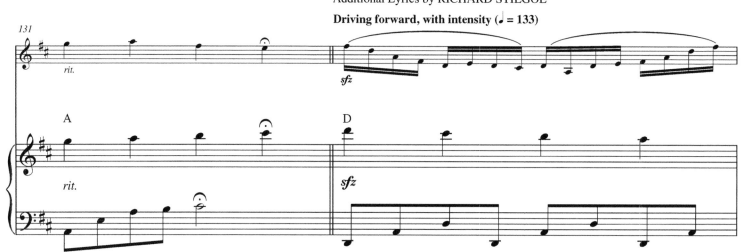

THE PHANTOM OF THE OPERA
Quicker, with intensity (♩ = 158)